D0918296

The Congress of Vienna was called to restore Europe to its old, traditional system of order, an order that Napoleon I of France had destroyed largely by force. It marked the end of a long period of wars between Napoleon and a European coalition of powers. It also provided for additional meetings of the major European nations to head off future wars. The congress was the beginning of a full century without a major conflict, and much of the credit for the lasting peace is given to the meetng at Vienna. Although its importance was diplomatic, the congress also discussed other matters, such as the international slave trade and the rights of river navigation in Europe. Because of its diplomatic accomplishments and the glittering personalities of its members, many of whom were royalty, it is known as one of the most outstanding international congresses in history.

PRINCIPALS

ALEXANDER I—Russian czar and founder of the Holy Alliance, whose extraordinary character changed the fate of the congress.

FRANCIS I—emperor of Austria, of the House of Hapsburg.

FREDERICK WILLIAM III—king of Prussia, who came to be dominated by Metternich.

BARBARA VON KRUEDENER—baroness whose deep convictions and strong character played an important role in the formation of the Holy Alliance.

LOUIS XVIII—king of France after Napoleon's downfall.

PRINCE METTERNICH—host of the congress and Austrian minister of foreign affairs, whose intelligence, personality, and character made a tremendous impact on all the attending members.

NAPOLEON I—ex-emperor of France.

ROBERT STEWART (later Lord Castlereagh)—British foreign secretary, leader of the House of Commons, and Britain's principal delegate to the congress.

PRINCE TALLEYRAND—outstanding diplomat and chief French delegate at the congress.

THE CONGRESS OF VIENNA

1814-15
The Diplomacy Surrounding
the End of the Napoleonic Era

By Emil Lengyel

A World Focus Book

FRANKLIN WATTS, INC.
NEW YORK | 1974

Photograph on title page shows one of the palaces used by the Congress of Vienna.

Cover by Nick Krenitsky
Map by George Buctel

Photographs courtesy of:

Austrian Information Service—pp. 7, 8, 30, 32–33, 36, 49, 52–53; Author—title pp., 20–21, 35, 48; Library of Congress—p. x; National Maritime Museum—pp. 26–27; New York Public Library Picture Collection—pp. 4, 12, 13, 16, 24.

Library of Congress Cataloging in Publication Data

Lengyel Emil, 1895–
    The Congress of Vienna, 1814–15.

    (A World focus book)
    Bibliography: p.
    SUMMARY: Discusses the purpose, members, and accomplishments of the congress called to restore order to Europe after the Napoleonic Wars.
    1. Vienna, Congress, 1814–1815—Juvenile literature [1. Vienna. Congress, 1814–1815. 2. Europe—History—1789–1900] I. Title.
DC249.L45   940.2'7   73–12440
ISBN 0–531–02169–6

Contents

The Congress
of Vienna

Preface

The Congress of Vienna has been called the "dancing congress," because dancing is just what its participants did from the day it began in the early fall of 1814 to its end in the early summer of 1815. It was far more than a dancing congress, however. Called to restore Europe to its old system of balance, it was a landmark, a dividing line, the end of the Age of Napoleon. It was also the beginning of an age of peace.

The Age of Napoleon had seen wars that were concentrated in Europe. For a century after the congress, there was peace. Not only did the Congress of Vienna write and seal the treaties of peace, but it also managed to prevent the outbreak of further major conflicts. It also introduced numerous reforms in human relations. Another feature of the congress was that it gathered together perhaps the greatest assemblage of crowned heads and titled dignitaries ever seen. Historians consider it one of the most important international gatherings in the history of man.

Beginning
with Napoleon

At the turn of the nineteenth century, the French Revolution had run its course. It had proclaimed the age of "liberty, fraternity, equality." In the wake of the Revolution arose a man who soon attracted world attention. He was born in 1769 on the island of Corsica, in the Mediterranean Sea, to a family of Italian origin; his name was Napoleon Bonaparte.

Because of Napoleon's background, people began to call him "the Corsican." Since he was short, he was also called *Le Petit Caporal* ("the Little Corporal"), even after he had become a general. Corsica was then, and still is, French, and so he made his career in France. He had served the Revolution and turned out to be a fantastically gifted soldier. At the age of twenty-five, he had won worldwide fame.

Napoleon as
Consul of France

1

Napoleon had bold ambitions for France and for himself. He wanted France to unify Europe. By becoming the ruler of France, he would, in effect, be the ruler of that continent. He reasoned that whoever ruled Europe might also rule the rest of the world. Partly by military skill and partly by political shrewdness, Napoleon gained control of France. In 1804 he was crowned emperor.

To fulfill his ambition of unifying Europe, Napoleon built the most effective fighting force of the age, known as *la grande armée* ("the great army"). The years from 1804 until the Congress of Vienna were a time of chaos, wars, and social disruption, as one man tried to force his will on all of Europe.

Napoleon recognized Great Britain as his chief enemy and Austria as his chief rival for European control. He planned to invade Britain and, with the help of Spain and the Italian state of Naples, to drive the British from their territory in the Mediterranean. These plans were ruined when the British defeated the French fleet at Trafalgar in 1805.

Elsewhere Napoleon, with diplomacy and military skill, was more successful. He established satellite kingdoms in the Netherlands, Spain, Westphalia, and Naples, controlled by his relatives. He made his son king of Italy in 1805. He extended the borders of France to include the Austrian Netherlands. He reorganized and controlled Germany, and caused Austria to lose much territory to him. Area after area fell—Hanover, Hamburg, Bremen among them. By 1812 it seemed as though all of Europe was destined to be under the French emperor's control.

But the years of war had cost the French dearly in men, materials, and money. French morale sagged, and the other European nations, waiting for a chance to overthrow the tyrant, were encouraged. In 1812 Napoleon marched his great army into Moscow, where the rugged climate and a determined defense by the Russian people defeated him. There his "great army" wasted away.

Although Napoleon raised another army and won more victories in Germany, the European nations now realized he could be defeated. They formed an alliance (one of several) and met his forces at Leipzig, in the German kingdom of Saxony, in October, 1813. Napoleon was the loser in the spectacular engagement known as the Battle of the Nations. The French forces were chased across Europe and into Paris. On April 11, 1814, Napoleon was forced to abdicate his throne.

Napoleon's second marriage, to Archduchess Marie Louise of Austria, daughter of the emperor, had produced one child, a son born in 1811. Now Napoleon proposed that the French throne be given to his son under a regency council.

Would the victorious powers accept another Napoleon on the French throne? Instead of deciding themselves, they turned the matter over to a French diplomat whom they trusted. Charles Maurice de Talleyrand-Périgord, Prince de Bénévent, had been Napoleon's grand chamberlain. Talleyrand, who had had many quarrels with Napoleon over the latter's aim of world conquest, did not decide in the emperor's favor.

Instead, Talleyrand proposed that the brother of Louis XVI, the Bourbon king who had been executed during the Revolution, be brought back from exile and given the throne. The Bourbons were not popular in France, a fact that the Allies realized, but they were the "legitimate" rulers, and this was the important issue. The Allies, who desired a return to the calm and order of Europe before Napoleon, were much concerned with legitimacy. This referred not just to rule "by the grace of God," but to government and institutions developed by time and tradition. This was a conservative approach, the opposite of revolutionary ideas. Revolutionists argue that change can bring

3

Louis XVIII enters Paris
as the new king.

a better world. Conservatives believe that change, at least rapid change, only destroys. Therefore, what is legitimate must be preserved. And because the Allies recognized the Bourbons as the legitimate rulers of France, they accepted Louis XVIII as the king.

The question of French succession settled, there remained the problem of what to do with Napoleon himself. The solution was exile to Elba, a small island in the Mediterranean Sea. Then a part of France (now part of Italy), Elba covers about eighty-six square miles. In 1814 it had only a few thousand inhabitants, who made their living by farming, fishing, and a little smuggling.

Napoleon's wife and son went to her father in Austria. The former emperor never saw them again.

Napoleon was out of the way and the legitimate French ruler was on the throne. But Europe was in chaos. The Allies wished to restore the Continent to its old system of order and balance, an order sanctioned by time and tradition. Toward this aim, the Congress of Vienna was called in the autumn of 1814.

The Congress
and Its Cast

Four major powers were represented at the Congress of Vienna
—Great Britain, Austria, Prussia, and Russia—as well as the
smaller European countries and states. It was the most impressive gathering of personalities, royalty, and diplomats yet seen.

The congress, which was in session for nine months, was
held in Vienna. The Austrian city was chosen as the site of the
meeting for several reasons. First of all, it was centrally located.
Second, it was the capital of a major power that had done much
to defeat Napoleon. It also was, and is, a most pleasant setting
for any gathering, situated at the foot of the softly rolling
Wienerwald (Vienna Woods) on the Danube, the largest river
of central Europe. The Austrian capital had the comforts of a
rich imperial city and the space to accommodate a large assem-
bly of crowned heads and their retinues.

Of all the glittering characters at the Congress of Vienna,
a few were especially outstanding and important. One was the

The city of Vienna

Austrian chancellor, Prince Klemens Wenzel Nepomuk Lothar von Metternich (1773–1859). So great was his influence on the congress and the period after it that an entire age was named after him—the time from the Congress of Vienna to the revolutionary upheavals of the mid-nineteenth century is called the Age of Metternich.

As shown in many paintings, particularly a portrait by the English artist Sir Thomas Lawrence, Metternich had strong features—an impressive forehead, full lips, blue eyes, and a slightly aquiline nose. He was a firm man to deal with but could also be gracious and charming. When he spoke, people listened with attention. While he had a remarkable capacity for work, he was also a "social butterfly." The contemporary pun in German indicates this: *Metternich-Schmetterling* (Metternich-Butterfly).

Later in his life Metternich had many critics, especially among the younger people, who considered him backward and a handicap to progress, but the Austrian prince was a man of great intelligence. He had witnessed the French Revolution, when the "masses ran wild"—as he saw it—and did not want to see such actions repeated. He thought that if left to themselves the people would return to savagery. He believed that only men of breeding and training had the capacity to govern. However, sometimes he did not trust even his fellow princes.

Prince Metternich believed in reason. Since revolution often led to war, chaos, and eventual dictatorship, he believed revolution to be unreasonable. He feared rapid change and preferred government proved by practice and time. Slow change would take place, of course, and was to be desired; rapid change

Prince Metternich, chief Austrian delegate
at the Congress of Vienna

was to be guarded against. He believed that the best interests of all peoples, whatever their nationalities or social status, were to be found in the maintenance of order and submission to authority.

One of the most effective organizations at the Congress of Vienna was the intelligence service of Prince Metternich. In truth, it was espionage. All correspondence, even letters addressed to the crowned heads, were first seen by Metternich's agents. His super-efficient valets and butlers, whose jobs were to serve the foreign rulers, were in reality spies in the pay of the prince.

Prince Metternich, a masterful man, in turn served his own master—Emperor Francis I, known to his people as *Franzerl,* which in Viennese affectionately means "Little Francis." Napoleon had stripped the Austrian leader of his former title of Emperor Francis II of the Holy Roman Empire. He became Francis I of Austria, a man of common sense who knew that his chancellor could take better care of affairs of state than he could.

Metternich represented the Hapsburg monarchy, a far-flung, old-fashioned empire, long in power but relatively weak compared to the other major countries of Europe. Above all, he wished to maintain peace and security throughout the Continent. He wanted to keep Austria in power in Germany (which was not then a unified country, but a number of separate states) and to keep Prussia from becoming the dominant German state. He did not want Russia to gain too much power, fearing that its strength could once again disrupt the Continent. And he wanted to keep Austria's power in Italy by returning to their thrones various rulers of the Italian duchies who would listen to Austria, and to Metternich. In all these things, he would prove remarkably successful.

Another outstanding figure at the Congress of Vienna was

the czar and autocrat of all the Russias, Alexander I (1777–1825). Pleasant and charming, he was head of the world's largest land empire, little known to the rest of the world. Some called him the revolutionary czar; to others he was a reactionary. Actually, as the product of a strange environment, he was both of these.

His father, Paul I, had been insane and was assassinated in the royal palace where Alexander lived. It was suspected by some that the son had known about the planned murder of his father.

In his youth Alexander was under the influence of a Swiss tutor, Frederic César de la Harpe, who was very modern for the times. The tutor made a great impression on the future ruler. After Alexander became czar, he toyed with the idea of many reforms. Socially, Russia was one of the world's most backward countries, mired in the institution of serfdom. Alexander entertained the idea of freeing all the serfs of his country, but he never did. He also considered many other modern ideas, which he seldom put into effect.

Several of the czar's fellow delegates thought that he was not as complicated as he seemed, but merely "confused." Others thought he was a mystic who lived a life withdrawn from reality.

Alexander I was interested in improving Russian strength and power in Europe through the Congress of Vienna. He was especially interested in obtaining Poland.

While Czar Alexander was the ruler of the largest country, the British representative, Robert Stewart, Viscount Castlereagh (he inherited the title of Marquis of Londonderry after the congress) represented the most powerful nation—Great Britain—and its global empire. As foreign secretary and leader of the House of Commons in London, he had been one of the principals in the coalition against Napoleon.

Castlereagh (1769–1822) was a handsome man and an

Left, Czar Alexander I of Russia

Above, in this famous scene of
the Congress of Vienna,
Castlereagh is standing directly
below painting. Standing to the
extreme left of the group is the
Duke of Wellington, who would
defeat Napoleon at Waterloo.
Metternich is standing in front of
his chair, and Talleyrand is
seated second from the right.

aristocrat; he was dignified, somewhat aloof, and seemingly shy in society. Metternich, who received detailed reports about him from his intelligence service, learned that the Englishman was taking dancing lessons in his Vienna residence to be ready for the congress. On Sundays he and his family gathered in their drawing rooms to sing Church of England hymns.

A brilliant man, Castlereagh was years ahead of his country in seeing Britain's role on the Continent. He was also ahead of any other British delegate in understanding the true nature and purpose of the congress.

The chief duty of the British foreign secretary was to guarantee that British superiority on the seas was not challenged in any way. He was also anxious to restore the European balance of power. No country besides Britain should receive too much, thereby increasing its strength. The heart of the British Empire —England—was, after all, a small island, which would be endangered by a powerful enemy in Europe. He wanted a balance that would keep peace and would keep aggressive powers out of the Continent. Castlereagh was tireless in his work, and he presented his country's case forcefully and with great success.

The head of the Prussian delegation was King Frederick William III (1770–1840). A famous portrait by Sir Thomas Lawrence shows him with a rigid face, not reflecting much intelligence. Indeed, he was said to be a most unintelligent and weak, if honorable, man. Frederick William, dominated by Metternich and influenced by Alexander, proved to be a bumbling delegate at the congress.

The Prussian king's aides were Prince Karl August von Hardenberg and Baron von und zum Stein. In his younger days the prince had advocated social progress and the extension of the common man's rights. The reaction in the wake of the Napoleonic wars engulfed him, too, and now he spoke in the interests of the princes and their way of law and order. While not of unshakable principles, he was a hard-working, competent diplomat. His colleague, Baron Stein, was a man of bolder vision. He wanted the Congress of Vienna to be the instrument of the unification of Germany, with Prussia as the major power. He failed in his attempt, and his failure was important. It meant that Austria could continue to dominate the German states, which it did until the second half of the nineteenth century, denying that power to Prussia. Both Metternich and Alexander considered any move toward German national unity as revolutionary. One of Metternich's brilliant accomplishments at the congress was that he convinced the German rulers that peace could be kept only through Austrian power.

Talleyrand (1754–1838), the chief French representative, qualified as one of the ablest diplomats at Vienna. (In fact, historians disagree as to who should be known as the greater diplomat at the congress—the Frenchman or Metternich.) Talleyrand was the son of an influential French aristocratic family, related to the French royal court. It was traditional in these families that the eldest-born male join the army, the national institution of prestige. At the age of four, however, Talleyrand fell out of a chest of drawers and was crippled for life. Therefore, when grown, he chose the next prestigious occupation, a high-ranking post in the clergy. Even though the young aristocrat was not religious, he took orders and became the bishop of Auton, a city in east-central France. A short time after, the Revolution broke out in France.

Promptly, Talleyrand took the side of the revolutionaries, who he thought were winning. Not only did he join the Revolution, but he also demanded that the state confiscate the proper-

ties of the Church. For that, he was excommunicated by the pope.

After a while, Bishop Talleyrand saw that the Revolution was getting out of hand. It executed the king of France. Extremists seized the reins of government and turned against even those members of the higher classes who were sympathetic to the revolutionary cause. Talleyrand fled Europe and went to the United States where he spent two years.

When he returned to France, the country was ruled by a Directory, a governing body that followed a policy of moderation. Talleyrand received a top position as the minister of foreign affairs. He quickly noticed that in the French armed forces, which were backing the Directory, was a young, fast-rising general—Napoleon. The general overthrew the Directory, became the first consul of France, and then its emperor. Talleyrand became Napoleon's chamberlain and was loyal to him as long as the emperor was winning. When luck turned against Napoleon, Talleyrand retired from public service, but continued to reside in Paris. He was always loyal to the winner, and, above all, he was loyal to his own interests.

Talleyrand was known to be a brilliant man and the most accomplished French diplomat. After Napoleon's defeat, Czar Alexander and other rulers sought his advice. He proposed that the legitimate ruler be brought back from exile. Louis XVIII, after his return to France, expressed his gratitude to the prince by making him the president of his council and his foreign minister. It was in this capacity, as the head of the French foreign service, that Talleyrand became the chief French delegate at the

Prince Talleyrand,
chief French delegate

Congress of Vienna. There he accomplished the most outstanding feat of his diplomatic career.

The French minister did, after all, represent a defeated country. However, he denied that. "It was Napoleon the Allies defeated," said Talleyrand, "not France." On the contrary, the France of Louis XVIII was Napoleon's enemy, and Talleyrand declared its place was at the victors' table. And that was where he took his seat.

Luckily for Talleyrand, the victorious Allies were quarreling among themselves when he arrived, somewhat later than the others, in Vienna. He became the peacemaker among the victors. Thus, it came about that at the Congress of Vienna, the chief delegate of the defeated nation sat with the victors and decided important issues. Thanks to Talleyrand (and to Metternich and Castlereagh, who did not believe in revenge, as Prussia did), France lost no territory at the peace conference.

This, then, was the situation as the Congress of Vienna opened: Europe had been torn apart and reorganized by Napoleon. Now the European powers wished to restore the Continent to its old, established order. They agreed on that. They did not agree on how this should be done, for individually they wanted different things. Metternich, Castlereagh, and Talleyrand, representing Austria, Britain, and France, did not want the balance of power in Europe to be upset. But both Prussia and Russia desired more territory and more power.

Almost immediately, the congress ran into trouble on this very issue. The disputes involved Saxony and Poland.

At that time, Germany consisted of thirty-nine independent states of varying sizes. Saxony was one of the largest. Its ruler, King Frederick Augustus I, had remained true to Napoleon when the other German rulers, headed by the Prussian

18

poleonic wars engulfed him, too, and now he spoke in the interests of the princes and their way of law and order. While not of unshakable principles, he was a hard-working, competent diplomat. His colleague, Baron Stein, was a man of bolder vision. He wanted the Congress of Vienna to be the instrument of the unification of Germany, with Prussia as the major power. He failed in his attempt, and his failure was important. It meant that Austria could continue to dominate the German states, which it did until the second half of the nineteenth century, denying that power to Prussia. Both Metternich and Alexander considered any move toward German national unity as revolutionary. One of Metternich's brilliant accomplishments at the congress was that he convinced the German rulers that peace could be kept only through Austrian power.

Talleyrand (1754–1838), the chief French representative, qualified as one of the ablest diplomats at Vienna. (In fact, historians disagree as to who should be known as the greater diplomat at the congress—the Frenchman or Metternich.) Talleyrand was the son of an influential French aristocratic family, related to the French royal court. It was traditional in these families that the eldest-born male join the army, the national institution of prestige. At the age of four, however, Talleyrand fell out of a chest of drawers and was crippled for life. Therefore, when grown, he chose the next prestigious occupation, a high-ranking post in the clergy. Even though the young aristocrat was not religious, he took orders and became the bishop of Auton, a city in east-central France. A short time after, the Revolution broke out in France.

Promptly, Talleyrand took the side of the revolutionaries, who he thought were winning. Not only did he join the Revolution, but he also demanded that the state confiscate the proper-

king, had deserted him. Prussia now demanded all of Saxony as its part of the spoils of war to punish its king.

In the same manner, Alexander wanted all of Poland for Russia. Actually, there was no nation of Poland any longer, although the Polish national sentiment remained. The country had been partitioned among Russia, Prussia, and Austria in the second half of the eighteenth century.

Great Britain and Austria, determined to preserve the balance of power, naturally opposed Prussia and Russia. Pledged to peace and unity on one hand, the four powers seemed ready to start a new war on the other. However, with the support of Talleyrand, Metternich and Castlereagh were able to bring about a compromise, and this maneuvering was among the most brilliant in the art of international diplomacy. It also saved the congress from disaster.

The dispute over Saxony was solved on the issue of legitimacy. Metternich successfully argued that Saxony was a traditional, legitimate state, and it could not be allowed to disappear. Talleyrand favored the legitimacy issue in order to keep his own country "as it had been." As a result, Prussia received a part, but not all, of Saxony, and the rest of the state remained in the hands of Frederick I.

Fearing Russian expansion into central Europe, Austria, Great Britain, and France were able to arrange a compromise with Alexander. Poland was repartitioned, with Russia receiving the part that came to be known as Congress Poland. It shared the rest with Prussia and Austria.

Over, Alexander's apartment
during his stay in Vienna

Using the issues of legitimacy and balance of power, the statesmen at Vienna were able, in a surprisingly short time, to bring order and peace to a continent that had been almost totally uprooted a short time before. Considering the differing ambitions and interests of each of the powers, their achievements were remarkable. The peace settlement at Vienna endured longer, with some minor changes, than any before or since.

The Congress of Vienna recognized the legitimacy of old ruling families—the Bourbons in France and Spain, the house of Orange in Holland, the house of Savoy in Sardinia. It restored territories to the German princes and, in central Italy, to the pope. Besides Saxony, Prussia received other German lands. In return for giving up claims to the southern Netherlands, Austria received the Italian territories it wanted, directly or through satellites. The colonies that Great Britain had taken during the Napoleonic wars—such as Ceylon and South Africa—were confirmed to the British. Sweden got Norway, and the northern and southern Netherlands were joined under the house of Orange. (This union, however, did not work, and some fifteen years later, split into the present countries of the Netherlands and Belgium.) Russia took over Finland. And France, the "defeated" country, lost no territory.

The Hundred Days and
the Dancing Congress

Late one night at the beginning of March 1815, Prince Metternich's valet awakened him. In the valet's hand was a diplomatic message marked "Urgent." It told the Austrian chancellor that on March 1 Napoleon had landed on the French coast, near the resort town of Antibes. He had escaped from Elba, bringing along his miniature army of 1,000 men. According to the latest reports, he was headed for Paris.

The crowned heads of the victorious governments acted quickly. The work of peace at Vienna was interrupted; the powers were ready to resume the war. They considered Napoleon Bonaparte an outlaw to be crushed by any means at their disposal.

Two main questions arose in the wake of Napoleon's escape. Would the French reject their present king and welcome the former emperor? And how could the Allies stop him? Russian and Austrian armies were, at the present time, returning to

The Battle of Waterloo

their homes. Only the British and Prussian forces were near France.

The answer to the first question came quickly. As Napoleon moved toward Paris, he was warmly welcomed by the French. The veterans of his "great army" rushed to join him.

On the evening of March 19, Louis XVIII, king of France, fled the city in secret. For the second time in his life he went into exile outside of France. The following morning Napoleon was carried into his throne room. France had become an empire again. And with skill and daring, the emperor reorganized the French army and led it northward.

The Allies, with the English forces in command of the Duke of Wellington, met Napoleon and his troops at Waterloo, a few miles outside of Brussels, today's capital of Belgium. On June 18, 1815, Napoleon lost the battle, the war, his throne, and his freedom. Today we still use the term, "He has met his Waterloo," when speaking of someone who has been defeated.

Declared an outlaw, Napoleon fled Waterloo and reached Paris, followed by Prussian troops who had orders to take him dead or alive. In the capital he tried once again to have his young son placed on the French throne. The Allies, however, decided that despite the cowardice shown by Louis XVIII, he was recognized as the legitimate king and should be placed on the throne once more. The period between Napoleon's entry into Paris on March 20 and the king's return on June 28 is known as the Hundred Days.

Napoleon managed to reach the French coast on the Atlantic, where he considered sailing to the United States as an escape. However, he finally surrendered to the British, who

Over, Napoleon surrenders
to the British and
is exiled to St. Helena.

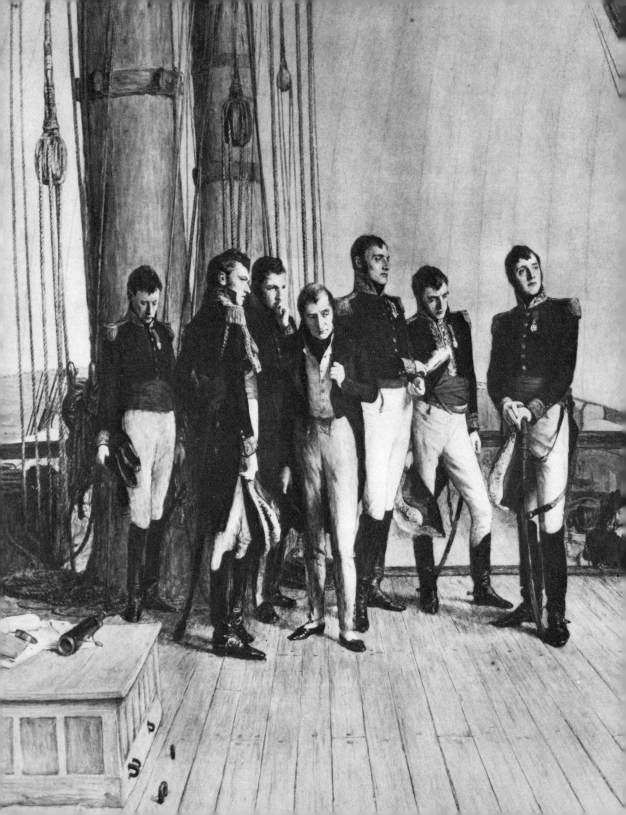

transported him to the tiny island of St. Helena in the south Atlantic. There he remained until he died on May 5, 1821.

The Congress of Vienna went back to work.

Napoleon had practically turned Europe into a French possession; nations were either directly governed by him, by his relatives, or by other rulers whom he had forced to serve his aims. As we have seen, the Congress of Vienna spent much of its time redrawing the frontiers of the Old World countries.

Talleyrand was successful in convincing the victors that Napoleon, not the French, should be regarded as the enemy. He was able to do so in part because Metternich and Castlereagh did not want a vindictive peace. Therefore, even after the Hundred Days, France was treated leniently. Its frontiers were retained, except for minor border changes. It was obliged to pay some indemnity to the Allies and to return the works of art that Napoleon had taken as spoils of his campaigns. But it certainly was not a vindictive peace settlement.

Napoleon had taken the first step in reuniting the German lands when he had set up the thirty-nine independent states. The Congress of Vienna took the second step by establishing a German confederation, within which each ruler retained sovereign power. The object was to enable the countries to get used to living together and to work out a solution for themselves. A Central Diet was set up in the city of Frankfurt to draft the fundamental laws of the confederation. The Diet had a complicated structure, consisting of a directory, in which authority was to be shared by Austria and Prussia, and two councils, in which the other German states and cities were to be represented.

Once again, in this matter of the German Diet, Metternich showed his subtlety and brilliance as a diplomat. The German Diet came to be dominated by Austria, not Prussia. The reason was Metternich. He was able to convince the German rulers that stability and peace for them could be maintained only with Austria, not Prussia, in control.

Among other serious problems confronting the Congress of Vienna was the slave trade. From the end of the Middle Ages, practically all the so-called civilized world had been engaged in such trade, mainly involving Africa.

The Congress of Vienna had no actual power to end the slave trade or slavery, but, led by the British, it did issue a statement condemning trade in slaves, saying that the practice was an evil one. (Denmark had ended its involvement in the slave trade in 1803, and Great Britain in 1808.) Later, with Spain and Portugal the only major countries still carrying on this commerce on a large scale, Great Britain paid huge sums of money to both countries to abolish slave trading north of the equator.

The delegates at the congress also took up the issue of anti-Semitism. A number of Jews had petitioned the meeting at Vienna to confirm the civil rights that Napoleon had granted to Jews in Germany. The Congress recommended that such rights be retained by the governments. It did not, however, come anywhere near to eliminating anti-Semitism. In eastern Europe, especially Poland and Russia, Jews continued to be treated as second-class citizens by their governments.

The congress also sought to unite Europe more fully by making river navigation easier. The rivers of Europe were the main arteries of transportation. The congress established the principle of free navigation on streams serving the trade of several countries. The most important of these were the Rhine and Meuse rivers.

The Congress of Vienna sincerely tried to solve—and to a remarkable degree did—the difficult problems of the times. The fact that such serious and complex issues were settled so well

Castle in Vienna where
some of the meetings took place

among nations with differing ambitions and interests marks this meeting as a truly—perhaps *the* truly—outstanding example of diplomacy in action. Yet, the task was not an easy one, and frequently the delegates became bogged down in what seem foolish and trivial matters (much like many international gatherings of today, where the question of who sits where takes up as much time as the problems before the group).

Not unlike modern diplomats, the ambassadors, representatives, and rulers at Vienna were all very insistent about their rights. Resplendent in magnificent uniforms and plumed hats, they would sometimes engage in rather undignified pushing and shoving to see who would enter a conference room first. At least twice, the race for the number-one position took on rather serious aspects.

On one occasion, both the coach of the Spanish ambassador and that of the French ambassador were heading toward the same function. The Spanish ambassador took offense because the other's coach was ahead of his. The Spaniard ordered his coachman to push the French coach out of the way. As a result, the two ambassadors ended up in a street brawl that nearly caused the two countries to break off diplomatic relations.

Before the nineteenth century, the Holy Roman Emperor held the highest titular rank. Therefore, the delegate representing this title occupied the head of the table at any international gathering. At one such meeting the French ambassador's seat was placed next to that of the Holy Roman Emperor. But the Russian ambassador arrived first and sat down in the seat reserved for the Frenchman. Naturally, the French ambassador

Over, one of the elaborate
meeting rooms for the congress

was outraged when he arrived. He demanded his chair. The Russian refused. So, the French ambassador took another chair and tried to squeeze it between the delegates of the czar and the Holy Roman Emperor. The incident did not end there since the Russian ambassador was challenged to a duel and was scratched in the process.

Other matters of diplomatic protocol got in the way of the work of the Congress. It had generally been a matter of great importance as to what country should be the first to sign a document. At times, as many copies were made of the documents as there were countries to sign so that every country could sign first. The Congress of Vienna solved this problem by declaring that the countries should sign international documents in alphabetical order of the nation's name in French, the language of diplomacy at the time.

Another problem was deciding who should enter a conference room first. (At times, international meetings had gone so far as to build several doors into one room so that everyone could enter at the same time.) More sensibly, the delegates at Vienna decided that a diplomat's rank should be determined by length of service in his present post, not the importance of his country. The longer he served, the higher his seniority, a rule still honored today.

But despite some undignified behavior, and other trivial matters that came up from time to time, the delegates were able to attend to the business before them. However, not all was work at Vienna, a fact that later lead to the phrase the "dancing congress."

It is not surprising that the delegates to the congress also wanted relaxation. Even though serious problems faced them, the delegates at Vienna knew that war was over and peace, if

The delegates enjoyed the beautiful palace gardens.

they could come to agreement, lay before them. It was a time for work, but it was also a time for celebration.

The official host of the congress, Emperor Francis, had appointed a festivals committee, which turned the majestic halls of the imperial residence, and elsewhere, into ballrooms. According to reports, some of the leaders never tired of dancing. The music was lighthearted and graceful. Especially popular was the waltz, Vienna's own special dance music, quite new at the time. The congress attended many orchestral performances, too. One of them was conducted by Ludwig van Beethoven. Besides the music and dancing, there were masked balls, hunts in the Vienna Woods, winter sports out of doors, and visits to the surrounding areas.

In fact, the entertainment program became so heavy at one point that some of the diplomats, inclined to be somewhat mistrustful, suspected that all this was a plot on the part of Metternich to wear them down. Even good-natured Emperor Francis found the schedule a bit tiring. "I can't stand this much longer," he complained half-seriously. "If it keeps going on, I shall resign."

In contrast to some of the ornate halls,
Emperor Francis I had rather plain quarters.

The Alliances

The aim of the victors after the Congress of Vienna was that there should be peace in the world. To insure it, they set up a series of alliances, the most unusual of which was the one called the Holy Alliance. Signed in September, 1815, at the end of the Congress of Vienna, the Holy Alliance sanctified the reign of the rulers of Europe. When those in power ruled, said the alliance, they did so by "the grace of God." And they acted in such a way that "legitimacy" (the old order) should be maintained. Any attempt to change it was thus not only treason against the monarch but also sacrilege against God. Under this system, the existing order could last forever. As history proved, however, it did not.

The beginnings of the Holy Alliance involved Czar Alexander and Baroness Barbara von Kruedener. Born in the city of Riga on the Baltic coast, the baroness spent the first forty years of her life caught up in the social and wealthy world of Europe.

But after forty she became involved with a religious group known as Pietists, who stressed repentance and regeneration, and with the so-called Chiliasts, who believed that Christ was soon to return to earth in visible form. She became a missionary, traveling from country to country telling people of the second coming of Christ.

About the time of the Congress of Vienna, the baroness had a vision. The so-called man from the north, who—in the words of the Prophet Isaiah—could bring peace to the world, was none other than Czar Alexander I of Russia, she said.

Baroness von Kruedener obtained an audience with Alexander in June, 1815, and was able to convince him that the fate of the world was in his hands. From the baroness's convincing speech and Alexander's already deep mysticism grew the Holy Alliance.

The treaty sounded far more like a religious tract than a diplomatic document. Its signers were to "consider themselves members of one and the same Christian nation . . . delegated by Providence to govern the three branches of the one family, thus confessing that the Christian world, of which they and their people form a part, has in reality no other Sovereign than Him, to Whom alone power really belongs, because in Him alone are found all the treasures of love. . . ." Also, the rulers pledged themselves to consider their subjects as their children.

The signers of the Holy Alliance may have meant what they said when they signed. But they interpreted the document to mean that since they ruled by the grace of God, their actions could not be questioned. They represented Divine Power on earth. This was, in reality, a good way to crush any stirrings of democracy.

When Emperor Francis of Austria read the treaty, he was

not sure whether it should be signed by his confessor or his chancellor. Metternich called it a "loud-sounding nothing," but he recommended that it be signed to "humor the madman" (referring to Alexander). Lord Castlereagh of Britain called the document a "piece of sublime mysticism and nonsense."

Just the same, the alliance was promptly signed by Austria, Prussia, and Russia, followed by other countries. Britain refused to sign on constitutional grounds, and the pope could not sign a document drawn up by a member of the Eastern Orthodox Church.

A main importance of the Holy Alliance was that through it Metternich was able to manipulate Alexander. Playing up the czar's mysticism, Metternich kept Russia fully on Austria's side and, therefore, was able to keep the balance of power as Austria wished it to be.

Despite the lofty intentions of the Holy Alliance, in later years it became more a symbol of repression than of peace. When uprisings broke out in Germany and Italy, for instance, against despotic rulers, members of the alliance helped to crush these revolts because they were considered "sacrilegious" —that is, they questioned the existing rulers, who were governing, presumably, as "Christian brothers" in the spirit of the Holy Alliance.

Of more political importance in preserving peace in Europe were the so-called Quadruple Alliance and other treaties during the next several years. They helped to cement what had been achieved at the Congress of Vienna.

The Quadruple Alliance of 1815 was signed by Great Britain, Prussia, Russia, and Austria (later joined by France to become the Quintuple Alliance). Its purpose was to regulate the political system of Europe and to supervise the outcome of the

NORWAY
AND SWEDEN

FINLAND

GREAT
BRITAIN

DENMARK

R U S S I A

• Moscow

0   200   400   600
Miles

ENGLAND

Hamburg
Bremen

HANOVER

NETHERLANDS

Brussels

P. WEST-
PHALIA

P R U S S I A

Warsaw •

CONGRESS
POLAND

Waterloo

Aix-la-
Chapelle

Frankfurt

LUX.

Leipzig

SAXONY

Troppau

CRACOW

Paris

FRANCE

Autun

SWITZ.

KINGDOM

BAVARIA

Danube

AUSTRIAN

Vienna

EMPIRE

HUNGARY

PYRENEES

ITALY

Laibach

ELBA

Verona

TUSCANY

PAPAL

STATES

OTTOMAN

PORTUGAL

SPAIN

CORSICA

OF

SARDINIA

SARDINIA

KINGDOM

OF TWO

SICILIES

EMPIRE

Cape
Trafalgar

M E D I T E R R A N E A N   S E A

GERMANIC CONFEDERATION

Europe
in 1812

EUROPE

1814-1815

Empire of the French

States allied with
Napoleon

States under Napoleonic control

G. Buctel

decisions made at the Congress of Vienna. Accordingly, members of the alliance held several meetings over the next few years.

The first meeting after Vienna was held at Aix-la-Chapelle (now Aachen, West Germany) in 1818. It settled the question of French war debts, wound up the military occupation of France, and admitted that country to the union of the great European powers.

The main trouble spots in Europe at the time were the Italian peninsula, the German states, and Spain. As we know, Austria received some of the richest parts of the Italian peninsula (namely Lombardy and Venetia), while most of the rest was assigned to members of the Hapsburg ruling family and other satellites of the Vienna court. But millions of Italians wanted one Italian nation (which they finally received half a century later), and they fought to gain their aims. In the same way, many Germans wanted a united nation under democratic rule.

The Allies met periodically to stamp out such movements, which would naturally have overturned the old order. They convened in 1820 at the city of Troppau (now Opava, Czechoslovakia) where they discussed how to stop the revolution in Naples. The following year they met in Laibach (today Ljubljana, Yugoslavia), where it was decided that Austria should crush the trouble in Naples, which it did. The British, at this meeting, refused to go along with such methods.

On October 20, 1822, the Allies met at Verona, Italy, to discuss what to do about Spain. (After this conference, Great Britain left the alliance.)

Spain at the time was governed by a tyrant, Ferdinand VII. During the Napoleonic wars, he had been stripped of his crown. The Spanish colonies in America had claimed freedom from Spain and had become independent.

Revolution now flared up again in Spain against the tyrannical king. By that time the alliance members, committed to the old order, were concentrating on defeating freedom-fighting movements. At Verona, the members decided to help the Spanish king to crush the revolution. Alexander volunteered to send an army of 150,000 into Spain, but the idea of regiments of Cossacks tramping across Europe did not appeal to the assembled diplomats. Therefore, Louis XVIII of France was asked to send an army across the Pyrenees to crush the revolution in Spain. The French king, who was not a brutal man, made the Spanish king swear on the Bible not to take revenge on the defeated foe. The revolution was crushed, and Ferdinand promptly broke his pledge with repressions that were bloody beyond belief.

Now the alliance could turn against the freedom fighters in the Spanish colonies, for revolution in Europe was not the only concern of the Allied powers. Any kind of revolution anywhere was not only treasonable but also sacrilegious, because it was directed against the majesty of law, incarnated in the monarchs, deputies of Christ on earth. In this way, both the Holy and Quadruple alliances became instruments of repression.

At the time of the meeting in Verona, James Monroe was President of the United States. He reacted to the Verona declaration in his message to the American Congress in 1823. Monroe declared, in the name of the United States, that the nations that had established their independence on the American continent were henceforth not open to control or further colonization by European powers. This became known as the Monroe Doctrine, a rather daring statement for a relatively weak young nation to make. It placed the Western Hemisphere out of bounds for Europe, declaring American responsibility for its independence.

Britain, now out of the European alliance, became the "silent partner" of the United States, supporting the Monroe Doctrine with naval strength. The British did not want Spain to regain its American colonies, not only because that would have upset the balance of power but also because of Spain's restrictive policies, known as mercantilism, under which the colonies' international trade interests were placed second to those of the ruling country overseas.

Although the alliance continued to exist for several more years, its power began to decline. Mainly the alliance operated to preserve the balance of power and to extinguish the flames of revolution throughout Europe. The leader in these causes continued to be Metternich, who feared revolution and the emergence of nationalism because he felt they would lead to an unbalanced Europe and to war. And in this he was right. His dominance of the European scene from the Congress of Vienna until the revolutionary year of 1848 is the reason that this period is known as the Age of Metternich.

The Fate of
the Main Cast

The glittering personalities at Vienna went their separate ways after the congress. Czar Alexander I, the man of mystery, became increasingly more involved in mysticism and increasingly more suspicious of those around him. On the way to the conference in Aix-la-Chapelle, an attempt had been made to kidnap him. Now he would trust no one. At home, his young daughter, an only child, died, and his wife became ill.

In 1825, ten years after the Congress of Vienna, the "Czar of All the Russias" died in the city of Taganrog. About five years before that, he was visited in his capital by Baroness Kruedener. Before he left Vienna, he had asked her to visit him at the palace in Russia. However, when she appeared at the palace and asked for an audience he refused to see her. Embittered, she and some of her followers traveled to the Crimean peninsula, in the south of Russia, where she died on Christmas Day, 1824.

After the official announcement of the czar's death, a

British ambassador at the Russian court said he had seen Alexander boarding a ship. It was later rumored that a monk in Siberia was really the former ruler. Whatever the truth, when the Soviet government opened Alexander's grave many, many years later, it was empty.

After the congress, Austria's Prince Metternich continued to be a strong influence in Europe. He gained even more power in Austria when Emperor Francis died in 1835. The emperor was succeeded by Ferdinand I, who lacked average intelligence and left control of the government to Metternich. In 1848, as revolutions swept across Europe to Vienna, Ferdinand was forced to abdicate. When he did, Metternich was forced to resign. He retired to London with his family. In 1851, with the revolutions crushed in Austria, he returned to Vienna where he was infrequently consulted by the new ruler, Francis Joseph I, Ferdinand's nephew. Metternich died in 1859 at the age of eighty-six.

Prince Metternich was a powerful and brilliant man. His mistake, if it can be called such, was that he tried to keep the Hapsburg monarchy as it was. Rather than adapt the monarchy to changing ways, he tried to preserve it as long as possible, which he sincerely felt to be his duty. In fairness it must be said that he had influence mainly in foreign affairs, less in the domestic problems of the monarchy.

Talleyrand also ran into trouble with his government. Made president of the council and foreign minister by Louis XVIII, he was forced to resign in late 1815 because the French nobles were jealous of him. However, he remained a personal favorite of the king's, who named him high chamberlain and granted him an annuity of 100,000 francs, a large sum at the time.

Another revolution broke out in France in 1830. This one ousted the ruling Bourbon family. Once again Talleyrand became the peacemaker. He persuaded Louis Philippe, Duke of Orleans, of the younger branch of the Bourbon house, to accept the French throne. As a reward, Talleyrand became ambassador to Great Britain, where he stayed until 1834. He died four years later at the age of eighty-four.

Many years later the secret archives of the Hapsburg family were opened. They revealed that Talleyrand had received rich fees from foreign governments for seeing that France signed certain treaties. However, these somewhat shady transactions seem to have been almost overlooked. "If he enriched himself," wrote one of his biographers, "he also helped to save France from ruin in more crises than one. In private life, his ease of bearing, friendliness, and, above all, his inexhaustible fund of humor and irony won him a large circle of friends." Even today, when speaking of the art of diplomacy, the phrase "he is a Talleyrand" denotes a statesman of great resource and skill.

Equally skilled as a diplomat was Great Britain's Lord Castlereagh. However, he began to suffer periods of depression after the Congress of Vienna. In 1822, as he was preparing to leave for the conference at Verona, to decide the fate of Spain, he cut his own throat. Castlereagh is buried in Westminster Abbey.

The Congress of Vienna convened in the great shadow of Napoleon. As we know, he was exiled a second time and died on May 5, 1821. From the time of his first exile on Elba until his death, the French emperor never saw his wife and child again. The Congress of Vienna granted the Empress Marie Louise a small country to rule in northern Italy. She eventually married again and outlived Napoleon by over half a century.

Left, Napoleon's young son sits
on the knee of Franz Joseph,
future emperor of Austria.

Above, room in the palace at
Vienna where Napoleon's son
died at the age of twenty-one

Napoleon's son was reared as a prince of Austria. While still in his teens, the handsome young man was given command of a Hungarian regiment. However, as the Austrian court physicians knew, he had tuberculosis, and he died of the disease in 1832 at the age of twenty-one. Although he had many titles and names throughout his short life, he is probably best known as *L'Aiglon* ("the Eaglet").

Conclusion

The Napoleonic campaigns had been long and devastating. The Congress of Vienna brought an end to that series of conflicts. After the congress, a few wars broke out from time to time, but peace was generally maintained for a full century. The arrangements produced by the peacemakers at Vienna are credited in part with this long peaceful spell.

After World War I in the twentieth century came World War II and others. The peace treaty of Versailles after World War I (1914–18) was not followed by generations of peace. What was the difference between the two peace conferences?

At the Congress of Vienna, France lost no territory and was not saddled with a heavy financial burden. After World War I,

Over, Vienna, shown here at the
time of the congress, was
the scene of one of the world's
great diplomatic meetings.

the treaties were harsh. The defeated countries were not invited but summoned to the conference table. They lost not only large territories, but were also saddled with great reparation payments.

In Vienna the delegates dealt with the problems in the way they thought best for their countries. In Versailles the statesmen were out to punish Germany. Nationalism had become a key factor in European life, and the delegates thought in terms of guilt, national punishment, and other determinations. In fact, the harshness of that treaty of Versailles is given as one of the causes of World War II.

Whether wholly successful or not, in its attempts at fairness and interest in the good of all, the Congress of Vienna may do well as a model of human decency. Perhaps it is here—in the contrast between Vienna and Versailles—that the biggest lesson for the modern world is to be learned.

A Selected Bibliography

Bartlett, Christopher John. *Castlereagh.* New York: Scribner, 1966.

Ferrero, Guglielmo. *Reconstruction of Europe: Talleyrand and the Congress of Vienna.* New York: Putnam's, 1941.

Freksa, Friedrich. *A Peace Congress of Intrigue (Vienna 1815).* New York: Century, 1919.

Kissinger, Henry A. *A World Restored: Metternich, Castlereagh and the Problems of Peace, 1812–1822.* Boston: Houghton Mifflin, 1957.

Lockhart, John Gilbert. *The Peacemakers, 1814–1815.* New York: Putnam's, 1934.

Nicolson, Harold George. *The Congress of Vienna: A Study in Allied Unity, 1812–1822.* London: Constable, 1946.

Index

About the Author

The city of Vienna and surrounding regions are familiar to Emil Lengyel, who was born and educated in Budapest, Hungary. After the secret archives of the Hapsburgs, the royal house of Austria, were opened to accredited scholars, the author was able to work in them. He also met some members of the Hapsburg dynasty, including Crown Prince Otto.

Mr. Lengyel has been a newspaper correspondent and has traveled all over the world. He is the author of a number of adult books, as well as numerous books for young people, published by Franklin Watts. His juvenile books include *Turkey, Siberia, Iran, Pakistan, Modern Egypt,* and *The Oil Countries of the Middle East* (all First Books), as well as biographies of Nehru, Gandhi, Asoka, Paderewski, and Kossuth, Hungary's great nineteenth-century patriot.

A resident of New York City, Mr. Lengyel is now in the social studies department at Fairleigh Dickinson University in Rutherford, New Jersey.